"All of us will face suffering at some point in our lives. In this brilliant and candid devotional guide Jeremy draws on his experience of an incurable cancer diagnoses to journey through the Bible with us. He offers 20 daily readings. What an encouragement to face up to fear and encounter Christ through his word. I highly recommend this as a practical resource in times of difficulty whatever you may be going through."

Dr Amy Orr-Ewing, President, OCCA The Oxford Centre for Christian Apologetics

"This pandemic has caused us all to wake up to the reality of suffering and death. It has posed the question, "Do I have a philosophy of life that copes with death?" Thankfully Jeremy Marshall helps us get the roof on before the storm hits. And please don't assume that he writes from some ivory tower, he has lived with an incurable cancer diagnosis for 5 years, so he has the credentials to walk us through the Bible's story of hope, which wonderfully assures us that the worst thing is never the last thing."

Rico Tice, Associate Minister at All Souls Church, Langham Place, Co-author of Christianity Explored

"Every human being will face suffering and death. Writing with searing honesty from the crucible of his experience with incurable cancer, Jeremey Marshall shares the sure and certain hope that can be found in Christ. These twenty short but profound meditations reflect on biblical characters and passages that remind us that, whilst we might not understand the reasons for our suffering, we have a good and wise sovereign God who has defeated death through the resurrection of Jesus, and who promises us an eternal glory that will outweigh all our suffering if we entrust ourselves to him. This book will comfort those enduring suffering, prepare those who are not yet suffering to face whatever lies ahead, and equip readers to bring

solid hope to the suffering. It will also serve as an excellent and accessible evangelistic resource to give to others."

John Stevens, National Director FIEC

"It needs knowledge of Christ to have words of empathy and wisdom for the world of sufferers. Sooner or later this will be a book for us all. Jeremy Marshall has surely been specially prepared to help us on the path he walks."

Iain H. Murray, Author

"This is a magnificent book. I already have a list of friends to whom I plan to send it. It will be an immense help and an encouragement to so many friends and relatives who are engulfed in fear and suffering."

William Taylor, Rector, St Helen's Bishopsgate, London

"This warm-hearted book of devotions has been forged in the fires of personal suffering. What has emerged is a series of reflections ranging across all of Scripture which acknowledges the tough times but points consistently to the Lord Jesus. Here is the medicine of the gospel dispensed with care and compassion. I warmly commend these short studies."

Revd Canon Angus MacLeay, Rector, St Nicholas Sevenoaks

HOPE
in the face of suffering

HOPE in the face of suffering

20 daily devotions
for tough times

Jeremy Marshall

First published in Great Britain in 2021

British Library Cataloguing in Publication Data
A record for this book is available from the British Library

ISBN: 978-1-913896-12-6

Designed and typeset by Pete Barnsley (Creative Hoot)

Printed in Denmark by Nørhaven

10Publishing, a division of 10ofthose.com
Unit C, Tomlinson Road, Leyland, PR25 2DY, England

Email: info@10ofthose.com
Website: www.10ofthose.com

1 3 5 7 10 8 6 4 2

Contents

Introduction

Perhaps the hardest part of the Christian life is dealing with the unholy and unwanted trio of visitors: fear, suffering and death.

Death, the Bible tells us, is the last enemy and we must all face it. Suffering usually comes before death and is a visitor we all dread. After all, who wants to suffer? Fear is normally the first of the trio to make our acquaintance, affecting our minds rather than our bodies.

Normally, of course, we don't like to think about these things. Suddenly, though, in the time of coronavirus, these unwelcome visitors cannot be avoided.

The French mathematician and writer Blaise Pascal was reported to have said, 'Being unable to cure death, wretchedness and ignorance, men have decided, in order to be happy, not to think about such things.'

But suddenly 'such things' are inescapable.

I have known this for longer than most. I have lived with cancer for seven years. Five years ago I was told the cancer was incurable and that my death was imminent. Since then I have been living with the sword of Damocles over my head. Now, however, that sword seems to be over everyone's head. While I was in chemotherapy it used to be just me who was nervous about coughs and sneezes. Now it's everyone. 'Welcome to my world!' I like to say, tongue firmly in cheek.

The truth is that despite their existence, Christians living in the developed western world have broadly been shielded from fear, suffering and death. This may explain why our faith is often so weak and feeble.

When I was a child, my father used to take our family Bible smuggling behind the Iron Curtain. When we visited those churches, I noticed that despite being terribly persecuted, the Christians we met had a vibrancy to their faith. Perhaps God is using the current crisis to teach us spoiled western Christians to live like Christians in the majority of the world who trust Him daily.

I'm reminded of the words that Corrie Ten Boom wrote in her book *The Hiding Place* when she recalled her time in a Nazi concentration camp, 'I only realised that Christ was all I needed when Christ was all I had.'

While I have been through chemotherapy, radiotherapy and other operations for cancer and blindness, I am not an expert on fear, suffering and death. I am not even – like my father – a clergyman. I am just a Christian, married with three adult children, living in the southeast of England, where I attend my local church.

I make this point only to say that these devotions are not about me but about three things that I have found we can use to defeat fear, suffering and death.

The first is that when we have a problem we must go to the Bible. The Bible is God's medicine cabinet where we can find treatment for our diseases. That is why each of the following devotions meditate on a Bible passage and considers how it can help us. I've chosen them because each passage has helped me powerfully over the last seven years and, in the same way, I pray that God will use His Word to speak to you. If you aren't familiar with the Bible, then there is some more information in the appendix about the Bible passages referred to in the devotions that I hope will be useful.

The second thing I have found is that when I read the Bible, God's promises come to life. These everlasting promises are like a rock upon which we can stand secure in the stormiest seas: 'Never will I leave you; never will I forsake you' (Heb. 13:5); 'Surely I am with you always, to the very end of the age' (Mt. 28:20); 'Even though I walk through the darkest valley, I will fear no evil, for you are with me' (Ps. 23:4).

God does not promise us health and wealth. That's the devil's lie. The writer in the letter to the Hebrews assures us of that when he writes that 'people are destined to die once, and after that to face judgment' (Heb. 9:27). There is no by-pass around the valley of the shadow of death. We all must go through it. In fact, we are called to take up our cross daily and follow Him. This can be unbearably hard, but there is something amazingly powerful in God's Word that enables us to endure to the end.

We may find partial theological answers to fear, suffering and death – and there is a place for that – but God's ultimate answer is Himself. A person who walked the dusty streets of Palestine and who was like us: facing fear, suffering and death. He can sympathise with our weakness and hardships because, amazingly enough, He experienced far worse. Christ never asks us to go through anything that He hasn't experienced Himself.

Yet, at the same time, He is *not* like us. He is God Almighty. He went to the cross because of His love for us. He holds the keys to death and hell. He can save us from fear, suffering and death. I am a living testimony that His presence can be experienced through His Word and my prayer is that you, too, will know His closeness as you look at His Word.

Thirdly, and finally, I have found that fear, suffering and death can be redemptive because in Christ we have hope. My cancer has been a powerful driver in motivating me to share my faith. I have written a book for non-Christians about the only real hope we have in the face of death. What do we have to offer in response to the coronavirus? Hope in Christ.

I have found that people are intrigued by the hope that I have. It is nothing particular to me; every Christian has the same hope. Jesus stands in front of us in our fear, suffering and grief and says, 'I am the resurrection and the life' (Jn. 11:25).

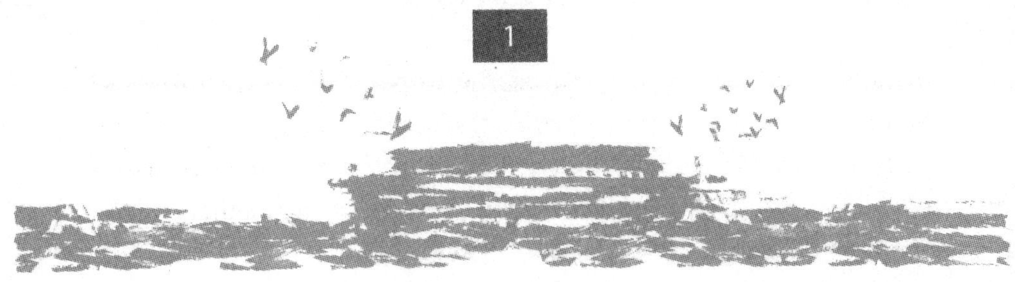

The Intruder

GENESIS 3

The Bible tells us that death and his two sidekicks, fear and suffering, are intruders. We are like a couple living in a beautiful house who, one night, hear the noise of breaking glass and suddenly realise that someone has broken in. We cannot get the intruder out and, sooner or later, he's going to kill us.

Sometimes the intruder breaks in because we live in a bad neighbourhood – the world is full of violent criminals like disease and natural disaster – but also, if we are honest, the intruder comes because of the moral evil within each of us. One sin leads to another and its destination is clear, 'the wages of sin is death' (Rom. 6:23).

You may have watched the popular TV show *Breaking Bad*, in which a respectable teacher becomes a drug dealer and unleashes a trail of suffering and death on everyone he comes into contact with. It's popular because it reveals something that we all know to be true.

So how did we end up being hired by this devilish employer? Or with this murderous intruder in our home? The Bible tells us that in the beginning the house – that is, the world – was good. How did moral evil enter the world? Genesis 3 teaches us that humanity suffered a catastrophic fall. Evil, in the form of a serpent, tempted Adam and Eve. They fell into sin and unleashed a wave of fear, suffering and death on themselves and their descendants.

This is the consequence of the Fall. The very first emotion the newly fallen couple experience is fear (Gen. 3:10). Adam and Eve suffered in specific ways (Gen. 3:16–19) but anyone who has been through childbirth or knows the hardship of work has experienced something of their suffering. And what's the end? Death. Back to the dust from where we came.

The damage is done. If you like, Adam and Eve were patient zero in a Wuhan wet market. Once the virus broke out it could not be stopped.

But wait! There is amazing hope: for as death came by one man, so life will come by another. And, strangely enough, that hope involves the same evil trio. From the woman, a deliverer will come who will kill that old serpent, the devil. He will obliterate the snake by stamping on his head but He will also have to suffer Himself. That rescuer, of course, is Christ, and the rest of the Bible is the story of how that happens. That story leads to a hill outside Jerusalem 2000 years ago, an old rugged cross and, near its foot, a new hewn tomb.

What comfort can we take from this? That God doesn't give us what we deserve. That God, before the creation of the universe, purposed a Saviour to save us from fear, suffering and death.

Since I was diagnosed with cancer I have spent a lot of time discussing with my non-Christian friends the question, 'How can a loving God allow suffering?'

The Christian answer to this question – and the answer to the unholy trio who afflict us so badly – is not a theological proposition.

Rather, the answer which we must share is a person. He is the Son of God who will crush fear, suffering and death. A man of sorrows who was acquainted with grief. He turns these three imposters on themselves. Even death, their terrible king, is utterly defeated and, as we will see at the end of this book, will one day be destroyed, '"He will wipe every tear from their eyes. There will be no more death" or mourning or crying or pain, for the old order of things has passed away' (Rev. 21:4).

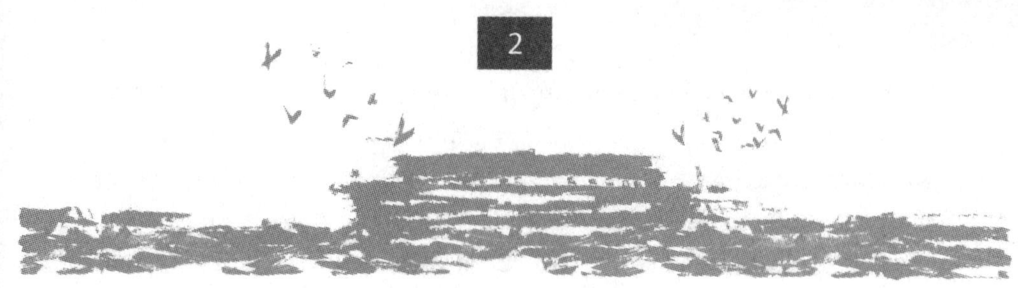

All Aboard

GENESIS 6 — 8

I spent much of 2020 in lockdown, either government-imposed or self-imposed, as I worried about coming into contact with Covid-19 with no immune system.

During that time, I felt as if I was being endlessly tossed around in a boat in a stormy sea, quarantined, cut off from others, fearful, lonely, wondering how long this would go on for and whether I would ever see 'dry land' again.

You don't have to be a Bible genius to see a passage that speaks to us — Noah and his ark. This is a passage that has been ruined by twee pictures of fluffy animals marching in two by two; the poor drowned corpses never seem to make it into the Sunday school illustrations.

What does it say to us then?

The story of Noah shows us that we live in a death-threatened world, whether we know it or not. Jesus tells us that people in Noah's day were living ordinary lives until suddenly everything changed. It's the same for us: in a few short weeks, in early 2020, our lives were threatened by something we had never previously considered. Without warning, we are alone on a stormy sea.

Where can we take comfort?

Firstly, from the great truth that God doesn't give us what we deserve. God was incredibly patient in the days of Noah and He is equally patient with us now. Not only is He long-suffering but, at the same time, He offers us a way to escape death. For Noah, it was the ark, for us, it's the cross. Both appear very unlikely routes to safety but all you have to do is 'get on board'. You don't need a golden ticket, there is room for all who will enter and all are invited.

Secondly, we read 'God remembered Noah' (Gen. 8:1). I sometimes feel forgotten as I lurch from one illness to another. Noah felt forgotten but of course, friend, God will never forget Noah, me, you or any of His children! 3000 years ago, God's people were saying the same thing: 'The LORD has forsaken me, the LORD has forgotten me' (Is. 49:14).

To which the reply came:

'Can a mother forget the baby at her breast and have no compassion on the child she has borne? Though she may forget, I will not forget you!' (v. 15)

No, in our suffering, pain and loneliness, we will never be forgotten. Nor are we ever on our own. Noah was not on his own; he had his family with him. We have our family — the church. Now, sometimes you may think that the church is the last thing you need in suffering, that it can be worse than useless or irritate you beyond belief. But the church is not as it seems: it is ultimately the body of Christ. As John says, 'Dear friends, since God so loved us, we also ought to love one another. No one has ever seen God; but if we love one another, God lives in us and his love is made complete in us' (1 Jn 4:11-12). In our church family, we are all brothers and sisters being made like our older brother, Jesus, as we are 'conformed to the image of his Son, that he might be the firstborn among many brothers and sisters' (Rom. 8:29). If we want to love Christ, whom we cannot see, we must first love our brothers and sisters, whom we can.

Ultimately, what we need in suffering, fear and death is Christ. He beckons us aboard His ship, the cross, of which He is both builder, captain and shipmate. He designed it, suffered it, offers it and is our companion and friend in entering it.

James K.A. Smith quotes Augustine, 'It is as if someone could see his home country from a long way away, but is cut off from it by the sea; he sees where to go, but does not have the means to get there.'

Smith continues 'You can't get there from here. Not even a map is enough. You might already have realized where you need to go, but the question is how to get there.' Augustine points out that God sends us an ark 'For no one can cross the sea of this world unless carried over it on the cross of Christ.' Get on board, says God, for the only way to reach home, is aboard the ark of the cross.

Thorns and Roses

GENESIS 37 — 50

Since I was diagnosed with cancer, I've never felt angry with God, but I've often felt bewildered and wondered, 'Why me?' I think we all feel something of this when we face fear and suffering.

In answering this question, I have found the story of Joseph to be helpful. It shows us very clearly that God's ways in suffering are mysterious and far, far beyond our understanding. In fact, it seems to me that the more I see of God's plans the more mysterious they are.

This shouldn't surprise us. In the book of Isaiah, God says, 'my thoughts are not your thoughts, neither are your ways my ways' (Is. 55:8). God doesn't ask us to understand what's going on; He asks us to trust Him. We are the clay and He is the potter.

One important truth that the story of Joseph reveals is that Christians should expect life to bring us thorns as well as roses. While Joseph wasn't perfect, in general, he tried to live a virtuous life. It would have been easy to give in to temptation when Potiphar's wife tried to seduce him. He rightly resists but is rewarded by being slung into prison.

The Lord Jesus invites us to take up our cross daily and follow Him. The prosperity gospel would have us believe that Christians should expect health, wealth and happiness. But that is no gospel. It is a lie from hell.

Through Joseph's experience, we also see that God's timing is perfect. By nature, I am prone to impatience. One of the things that I believe God is trying to teach me in illness is patience. From the moment he entered slavery to his dramatic revelation before his brothers, Joseph had to wait twenty-four years. How many times must he have longed to be free? Especially after he had helped Pharaoh's cupbearer interpret the dream, only to be forgotten by the man he had helped.

In his excellent book *Mysterious Ways*, David Kingdon points out that Joseph must have eagerly expected the key in his prison door and his moment of release. But for two long years, nothing happened. Yet, in a strange way, isn't that encouraging? The cupbearer had forgotten him, but God had not. Nor will God ever forget us, even when we are in the dungeon of suffering.

Finally, we see in Joseph's life that God often turns evil for good. As his brothers plead for his mercy, he reassures them, 'you intended to harm me, but God intended it for good' (Gen. 50:20). In this moment we see that Joseph is a type of, or signpost to, Christ. Like Christ, he was betrayed by his brothers, sold for thirty pieces of silver, unjustly sentenced and resurrected from prison to be the saviour of multitudes.

I find this so helpful. The cancer cells that are meant to harm me, I believe, God is using for good. I have had more opportunities to read the Bible with friends as I have more time and many of them are intrigued by my experience. Suffering makes us vulnerable and vulnerability can open people up to hear about the Saviour. The same may be true for you. We may not understand what has happened to us, but we can be sure that we are all part of God's plan. I believe that we will only know what part we play when we meet Him face to face.

Ultimately we, like Abraham, can rely on God's character. 'Shall not the judge of all the earth do right?' Only in heaven will we get an answer to this, but then everything will drop into place and we will fall to our knees in love and amazement.

As the hymn says:

With mercy and with judgment
my web of time he wove
and aye the dews of sorrow
were lustred by His love

I'll bless the hand that guided
I'll bless the heart that planned
when throned where glory dwelleth
in Emmanuel's land. [1]

One day we will bless the hand face to face. In the meantime, we must, like small children, place our hand by faith in the hand of Almighty God.

1 Anne Ross Cousin, 'The Sands of Time are Sinking', 1860.

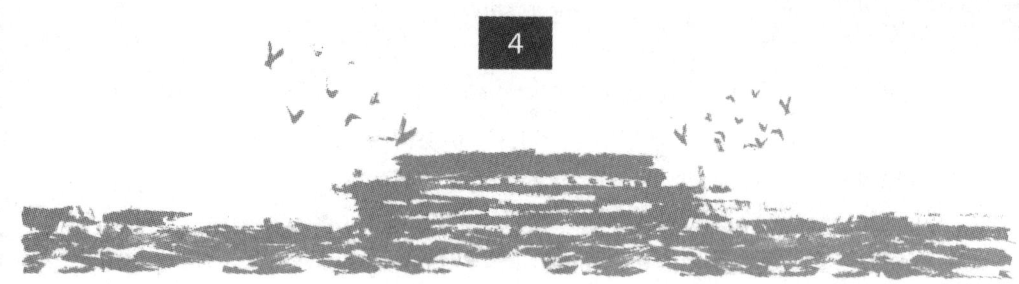

4

The Best Medicine

JOB 1 — 42

The book of Job shows how not to help others who are suffering. Job's comforters get so many things wrong. They try and take control. But if the storm is raging, only God can calm the storm. Our role is not to take hold of the tiller and try to steer the boat, but to be in the boat with our friend.

Everyone feels pain and suffering in a different fashion, which means it's dangerous to use generalities (as Job's friends do). God is a personal God who deals with His children in equal but individual ways. God has no one-size-fits-all. Sometimes all that can be done is to be quiet and listen.

We tend to shy away from people in suffering because we feel awkward and embarrassed, but actually, we need to overcome this feeling and reach out to them. It's also fine if – as may well be the case – we don't know the answers. Sometimes just our presence is helpful.

Weeping and crying is a good thing to do: Jesus wept at the tomb of His friend Lazarus. We may feel it's unbiblical to cry, but grief is godly and natural. Our culture doesn't like mourning, but Jesus was a 'man of suffering, and familiar with pain' (Is. 53:3). In the process of walking through pain and suffering it is not up to us to tell the sufferer when they are done. Sometimes people will never stop grieving, but as Colin Smith helpfully says, 'God gave His people a counsellor who wept with them, put the pain of their loss into words, ministered to their guilt and grief, and brought hope and healing from the ashes of their loss'.[2]

The variety of suffering which the Bible covers include suffering from natural disasters, suffering caused by others, suffering from disease, suffering from relationships, suffering brought on by ourselves, and many more. So, what is the best medicine?

I have found it to be God's Word. If we can do nothing else, we can certainly read a short Bible passage to a suffering friend. If you're short of ideas, then I would suggest the Psalms, which cover the whole range of human emotions. These words were prepared by God thousands of years ago and have been used ever since to provide comfort in times of need and suffering.

Sometimes the Psalms don't give us an answer to our pain. Psalm 88 ends bleakly, without even a hint of an answer, let alone a happy ending. But that's true of life sometimes. The Bible doesn't flinch from reality and it doesn't always wrap things up neatly.

Job shows us that we can tell God if we feel angry or upset. God is able to cope with our emotions. It is very striking that Job is angry with God. He goes well beyond what might be considered reverent or proper, yet at the end of the book it is his comforters who are rebuked, 'You have not spoken the truth about me, as my servant Job has' (Job 42:7), God says. We need to get over the feeling that we can only help if we are strong. Actually, suffering will impact all of us – we are all sufferers – we all need Christ's presence.

---

2 Colin Smith, *For All Who Grieve* (10Publishing, 2020), p. 105.

Sometimes there is little or nothing that we can do except pray. Prayer is a wonderful privilege. The old hymns say it well:

Oh what needless pains we bear
all because we do not carry
everything to God in prayer.[3]

Being available for people is important, especially over the long term. Sometimes people feel stigmatised. Dr Paul Brand, who was an orthopaedic surgeon who treated people with leprosy, tells a moving story about a badly deformed person who nervously visited his local church. A regular just patted the space next to him on the pew, indicated that he should come and sit there. The simple act deeply touched the suffering man.

Job is continually looking for a friend, an advocate, someone to represent him. We now know that he was looking for Christ.

God's ultimate answer to suffering is not a philosophy or even theology, but it is a person. When nothing else makes sense and nothing else is left, He is there and He will hold us fast.

This also means that if we are not sure what to do, then we can't go far wrong if we follow Christ's example in dealing with suffering, above all, in showing compassion. James says, 'As you know, we count as blessed those who have persevered. You have heard of Job's perseverance and have seen what the Lord finally brought about. The Lord is full of compassion and mercy' (Jas. 5:11).

---

3 Joseph M. Scriven, 'What a Friend We Have in Jesus', 1855.

5

The Crook in the Lot

'Consider what God has done: who can straighten what he has made crooked?' (Ecc. 7:13). The Scottish church leader Thomas Boston wrote a wonderful book on suffering, or, as he called it 'the crook in the lot', which I have found amazingly helpful. Boston was a pastor and lived a very obscure life in Ettrick, a tiny place in the Scottish Borders. He was well acquainted with suffering and the book is permeated with deep wisdom from the many sufferings that came into his 'lot'.

His church was hostile towards his ministry and deeply divided. His wife, Catherine, was a chronic depressive. Of their ten children, six died in infancy. They had already buried one child called Ebenezer (which means, 'Up to now God has helped us') when they had another son. Should they risk calling him Ebenezer also, given the tragically ironic nature of the name if he also died? They did name him Ebenezer and he also died.

What does Boston have to say? Boston argues that God deliberately allows each of us to have a 'crook', that is, something that pains us or causes us problems in our 'lot', that is, our life. God often causes this special trial to be the very thing that most rivals Him in our life. So, for example, if we are proud and self-sufficient then it might be a dangerous illness that makes us trust in Him and realise our own helplessness.

Think of the rich young ruler whom Jesus commanded to sell all he had. Jesus knew that money was the thing keeping him from faith.

God, the loving Father, trains us as a father trains his children to be more like Himself. He causes us to be aware of the sin that is in us and needs removing. None of this means that we suffer because we have been particularly sinful. That may be so, but Boston argues the exact opposite: that *all* Christians will find a 'crook in their lot'.

What's the remedy? Firstly, praying for God to help. If God put the crook in then He can take it out. He is intensely loving and sympathetic to us in our sufferings. 'As a father has compassion on his children, so the LORD has compassion on those who fear him; for he knows how we are formed, he remembers that we are dust' (Ps. 103:13–14).

God uses our crooks to draw us to Himself, to make us pray. I find that true in my own life. God may want to straighten us rather than straighten the crook. If God is speaking to us through our suffering, we need to first listen to what He says, while praying that He will remove it. We must not confuse this with fatalism. We are not helplessly swept around by the currents of life, like a leaf on a river, but are being expertly steered by a helmsman who loves us and died for us.

We need faith and humility. Faith, in that we believe that suffering is *not* random, but that God has a purpose in all that happens to us. 'A wise eyeing of the hand of God in all that we find hard to bear,' as Thomas Boston describes it.[4] For some of us, that truth is very hard to

---

4 Thomas Boston, *The Crook in the Lot* (Banner of Truth, 2017), p. 2.

understand. For some of us, it may only be when we meet the Lord face to face that we finally understand it.

And above all we need humility. Perhaps the most used verse by Boston is, 'Humble yourselves, therefore, under God's mighty hand, that he may lift you up in due time. Cast all your anxiety on him because he cares for you' (1 Pet. 5:6–7). Both verses are linked. If we realise that God is the God of the whole universe, that we, in the cosmic scheme of things, are utterly nothing but weak and sinful creatures, then we will see God as He is and ourselves as we are, and, as a result, we will come to God in our time of need for help and will find Him full of mercy.

God, most of all, wants to make us like Jesus. He went through the most terrible crook of all. He, despite being sinless, suffered on the cross for our sins.

God on the Throne

2 KINGS 5

We often don't know why illness happens. But we do know this: that God is sovereign over all things and is working everything together for His purpose. He reached Namaan, the commander of the Syrian army, Israel's public enemy number one, through a disease. Ultimately, Namaan came to realise that there is only one God in the world – the Lord the God of Israel.

God is always in control and working to bring about His will. This is true in every area of life, from geopolitics to finance, and pandemics to personal circumstance. God allows terrible evil to happen, but He may also use that same evil to achieve His purpose. The greatest example of this is Jesus's death on the cross, which the devil intended to use to destroy the Son of God but was actually the means whereby God liberated His people.

There are two alternatives. Either God is regulating the affairs of humanity or events just happen at random. The Bible leaves no room for uncertainty on which of the two is true.

Just after The Great Depression, A.W. Pink wrote that:

> *The Bible affirms again and again that God is on the throne of the universe ... that every day God is ruling and reigning. Without doubt a major crisis is at hand and everywhere men are alarmed. But God is not. He is never taken by surprise. It is no unexpected emergency which now confronts Him ... Although the world is stricken the word to the believer is 'fear not'. All things are moving in accord with his eternal purpose.*[5]

Naaman was a great man *but* he had leprosy.

Where is the gospel in this terrible disease? In a highly unlikely source: a little slave girl. She was snatched from her family – presumably, they were God-fearing otherwise how would she know what to say to Naaman? It's reasonable to assume that her family was killed – parents don't usually let their children be sold into slavery without force. Surely this could not be part of God's sovereign plan? Someone so weak and defenceless. Someone so insignificant that she doesn't even have a name!

But it's true. She was part of God's sovereign plan to turn evil for good. To this disease-ridden world, He sends ordinary, obscure, suffering Christians armed with the wonderful message of hope.

God allows His people to experience evil and suffering but, at the same time, it is our responsibility to react in a way that honours Him. Now, that's very hard – as I know from my own experience. Humanly we can't do it. Which is why we need God's help.

Think about the slave girl. What was her attitude to Namaan's illness? It wasn't: 'At last, God is punishing these wicked Syrians for enslaving me.' It wasn't: 'It's not my problem.' It wasn't: 'My God is for Israelites only.' It wasn't: 'I can't do anything.'

---

5 A.W. Pink, *The Sovereignty of God* (Baker Books, 2000), p. 14.

Rather, wonderfully, it *was* to have love and compassion for her enemy: 'If only my master would see the prophet who is in Samaria! He would cure him of his leprosy' (2 Kgs. 5:3).

She took a huge risk. We know this from the greatest Bible teacher of all time. The Lord Jesus tells us in Luke 4:27 that this was the first cure of a leper in that time. What courage this girl had! If she could recommend the prophet Elisha then how much more we can recommend one far greater. This is the answer when people ask us for help.

Christians should expect to suffer. If you are not suffering, thank God for the unusual time in which you find yourself. We must love the suffering people around us and tell them, 'If only you would seek Jesus of Nazareth! He will cure you of sin and evil.'

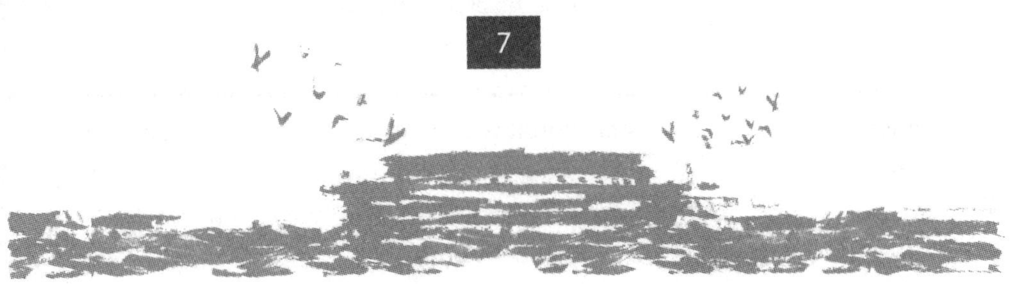

7

The Rollercoaster

PSALM 16

To what may we compare fear, suffering and death? To a rollercoaster. This is not an image we find in the Bible, of course! But, like a rollercoaster, when we suffer it can feel like we are strapped in and unable to get out. At times nothing much is happening and then suddenly you are thrown around, upside down and sideways before it stops equally as suddenly. Then the whole thing abruptly happens again. How do you feel when you get out? You are shaken up and your legs feel like rubber.

All of this has been my experience recently. Last week I started feeling unwell, then I developed a fever and by Sunday evening I had tightness in my chest. A few days later I was admitted to hospital either with coronavirus or some kind of heart problem. Various tests later and I am home, having had neither coronavirus nor a heart attack but some other unspecified illness.

The Psalmist writes, 'I will praise the LORD, who counsels me; even at night my heart instructs me. I keep my eyes always on the LORD. With him at my right hand, I shall not be shaken' (Ps. 16:7–8).

When we are bewildered and in trouble and wonder where the rollercoaster is going, God gives us His counsel. When we feel lost and abandoned, God knows where we should go and shows us the right path. How does God counsel and advise us in difficulties? In many ways, but most of all through His Word which teaches us in our hearts. In Hebrew, our hearts translates as 'my kidneys' which speaks specifically of our inmost being or essence.

As we are helped and taught, our eyes go away from ourselves. In difficulties, I find it easy to be self-absorbed. But our eyes must look up, not down, and look to Jesus. And as we look to Him through His Word we realise He is not someone to look at but someone who is with us – at our right hand.

If in ancient Israel, you wanted someone to protect you, you would place a mighty-armed warrior on your right side. That way you would be invulnerable. It's the same with us. As the rollercoaster takes another lurch up or down, seated next to us is someone who 'sticks closer than a brother' (Prov. 18:24).

Being ill or suffering often involves being lonely. In the hospital, I couldn't leave the room. But in isolation, we are never alone for He is with us.

Some might be tempted to think that this train of thought is typical of a weak human being who needs an imaginary friend in distress. We may feel happy, but is He real?

The Psalmist helps us by writing:

> *Therefore my heart is glad and my tongue rejoices; my body also will rest secure, because you will not abandon me to the realm of the dead, nor will you let your faithful one see decay. You make known to me the path of life; you will fill me with joy in your presence, with eternal pleasures at your right hand (Ps. 16:9–11).*

These verses were quoted by Peter in his Pentecost sermon to prove that Jesus was the Messiah who has come back from the dead. Ultimately the rollercoaster is terrifying because we know what's waiting for us at the end – death. But Jesus has beaten death, He has risen back to life, and so will we. Our hope in fear, suffering and death is unshakable and founded on the historical fact of the resurrection.

As we get off the rollercoaster our legs may feel like jelly and, if left to ourselves, they will buckle and we will fall. But the glorious truth is that we are not left to ourselves because the Lord Jesus Christ is at our right hand. He takes us by the arm and steadies our weak knees. He has conquered death and He will bring us home to His right hand where there will be no more fear, suffering and death, only joy and eternal pleasures forevermore.

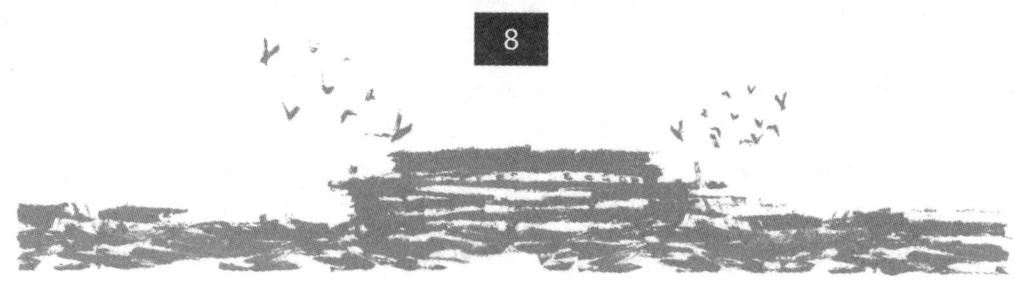

In His Hand

PSALM 31

Last October I was stunned by the news that two great friends of mine, Chris and Susanna Naylor, had been killed in a terrible car accident, taking them immediately to God, but leaving behind three children and so many grieving friends. And their death was while they were serving the Lord, with the wonderful Christian environmental charity A Rocha. The founder Peter Harris was badly injured and his wife Miranda killed in the same tragedy.

How very strange that Chris, who was my roommate from university, and a wonderful Christian and human being, should go to be with the Lord before me, when over the past few years he had been so kind to me when I thought I would die in a few months. How mysterious and strange are the ways of God. Life appears so uncertain and seems random. The future seems very fearful.

But then again as I pondered this, my mind was once again cast back to the Bible, to a verse in Psalm 31 which simply says,

But I trust in you, Lord
I say, "You are my God."
My times are in your hands.

I found this verse very helpful when I was first diagnosed with incurable cancer.

We worry about our times – how long will we live? Will I survive this illness? We, as it were, stare at the future and try and get on top of it. But friends, this is ludicrous. We are not able to control even a minute of our times, nor even to see an hour ahead, let alone change our destiny. Being ill exposed for me the truth that was always there but which I didn't like to think about: I control virtually nothing.

So are we at the mercy of blind fate? Is it like we are simply rolling the dice? Sometimes the dice come up with a good outcome – good health, let's say – and other times they throw us cancer. Every day 40–50 billion of our cells are replaced and sometimes that replacement process goes wrong. It's all completely random and there is no 'hand'.

The Psalmist rejects both outcomes. We note that he starts with trust. Belief in something implies that it is trustworthy. We put our lives in the hand of our doctors and oncologists because we trust that their actions will do us good. The more we get to know them and their skills the more we trust them. It's the same with God. We start with trust in Him (belief) but in fact, did we but know it, we are simply confirming the reality of something that's been true all along: that God has us in His hands.

How comforting it is that we (if we are His children) are in the hands of a trustworthy and loving Father. A good shepherd who loves and leads us along life's troubled paths. (Far less pleasant, of course, is the thought that we are in His hands but we are not His children. If that is you, come into the family of the Creator God who loves you.)

C.H. Spurgeon sums it up this way:

> *Yes, God considers our times, and thinks them over; with his heart and soul, planning to do us good. That mind that made the universe, out of which all things spring, bows itself to us; and those eternal wings, which cover the universe, also brood over us and our household, and our daily wants and woes. Do you believe that God's hand is working with you and for you? We feel we are immortal till our work is done; we feel that God is with us, and that we are bound to be victorious through the blood of Jesus. We shall not be defeated in the campaign of life, for the Lord of hosts is with us, and we shall tread down our enemies. God will strengthen us, for our times are in his hand; therefore we will serve him with all our heart, and with all our soul. He that takes care of our times, will take care of our eternity. He that has brought us so far, and wrought so graciously for us, will see us safely home.*

Given all this, how then should we live? I like good old George Whitfield's saying 'Until Christ calls us home, we are immortal.' As best we can, even though grieving and labouring and at times our eyes full of tears we can stumble along as long as we 'put our hand in the hand of the man who stilled the waters ... the man who calmed the sea'.

That man from Galilee holds our times and He holds us. Indeed He will see us safely home. Trust Him!

The Undistracted Parent

PSALM 34

Psalm 34 was written when David was desperate. It helped me when I was desperate.

The key thing in starting to know God is a sense of our need *for* God. This need is itself planted by God in our hearts, often, though not always, through suffering and pain. When we realise our own desperate situation then we turn and look to God. If we think everything is fine then why bother?

I find this extremely useful because when you are seriously ill the ultimate 'fallback' is God. I don't understand why God allowed my illness to happen but, nonetheless, I must and I will trust in the Father that He knows best.

Where must we start when we suffer? Though it can be very, very hard, we must never forget to say, 'Thank you', and tell others about God. The Psalm makes this plain, 'I will extol the LORD at all times' (Ps. 34:1). At all times, but most of all in times of great suffering and trial. Christians must also tell others how God has helped them. It is our responsibility, however difficult we find it, to tell others how great God is!

Notice the words that David uses, 'I sought the LORD, and he answered me; he delivered me from all my fears' (Ps. 34:4); 'This poor man called, and the LORD heard him' (Ps. 34:6); 'The eyes of the LORD are on the righteous, and his ears are attentive to their cry' (Ps. 34:15).

God is like a parent straining to hear a crying baby. He is highly attentive to our prayers. Both His eyes and His ears are attuned to us. God is not like us. We fall asleep and forget things. I am easily distracted and once even lost a friend's young son on a busy beach! But the Lord God Almighty is not like us. Ceaselessly, unwaveringly, every second of our life, His eyes are on us and His ears are listening to our cries. What must we do when we are in trouble? We must cry to Him for help in prayer and hear His voice through His Word.

James Montgomery Boice says of Psalm 34:

> *David's circumstances did not change. He was still a fugitive, still in danger, still alone. But God had preserved his life ... prayer does not mean God will change every difficult thing, but he will preserve you as long as he has work for you to do and will transform the most difficult circumstances by his presence.*[6]

I know this is true because He has done that for me.

This true and certain hope will deliver us from our fears. I am not ashamed to say I was and still am afraid, just like David. But God is with us if we trust in Him. 'The angel of the LORD encamps around those who fear him, and he delivers them' (Ps. 34:7).

Many Christians (though I don't think we can be absolute about this) argue that appearances of the angel of the Lord in the Old Testament

---

6 James Montgomery Boice, *Psalms: Volume 1* (Baker Books, 2005), p. 292.

were manifestations of the Son of God before His incarnation. Whatever the case, it is clear that the angel of the Lord promises to stay with us, actually to camp with us and around us and be with us every day of our life. This promise is renewed directly by the Lord in the New Testament when He says, 'And surely I am with you always, to the very end of the age' (Mt. 28:20).

The verse reminds us of the story of Elisha in Dothan. His terrified servant, full of fear and surrounded by enemies, has his eyes opened and sees the hills around him full of the armies of the Lord. Elisha comforts him by saying, 'Don't be afraid ... Those who are with us are more than those who are with them' (2 Kgs 6:16). May our eyes too be opened to the way in which the angel of the Lord daily encamps around us on all sides.

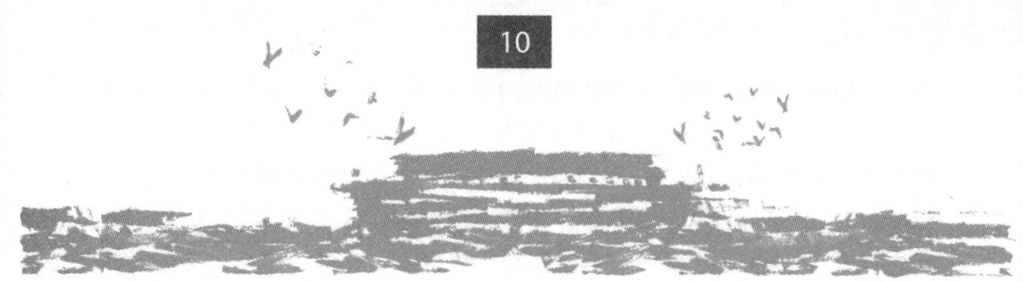

Rock in a Sea of Troubles

PSALM 61

As I write, I am looking down onto the historic streets of London from the Royal Marsden Hospital. I am here, as I alluded to earlier in the book, because I started to feel unwell with coronavirus symptoms.

One constant I have found in trying to cope with fear, suffering and death is that God speaks to me at my low points personally through His Word. Now, this can be overdone and, especially in our individualistic culture, we can easily take everything in Scripture as being about us directly, when really the big topic of the Bible is God. Nevertheless, I believe we sometimes, in fear of this, go to the opposite error, which is to treat the Bible as a theological textbook. It is not. It is a living, breathing, supernatural book of books, which speaks powerfully and personally this very day to each one of us.

Every time I have been in trouble in my illnesses it's as if the lights suddenly go and you notice intense light streaming out of the darkness. The light – God's Word – was there all along but the darkness makes it shine and the darker the night the brighter the light. We must delight in this light, for it will lead us in the dark. Indeed, we are explicitly commanded to do this for, as the Psalmist declares, 'Blessed is the one ... whose delight is in the law of the LORD' (Ps. 1:1–2).

Many of those moments of delight have come in the very hospital in which I am writing. Radiotherapy treatment is long and tedious and every day you must lie without moving so I decided to learn Psalm 34 by heart. I was going through it in my mind to memorise it while being treated and came to verse 5, 'those who look to him are radiant', which I suddenly realised is literally what was happening to me. I started laughing only to get told off by the radiotherapist for moving!

This week, as I worried about my strange illness, a friend mentioned Psalm 61 to me and another verse suddenly launched itself off the pages. 'From the ends of the earth I call to you, I call as my heart grows faint; lead me to the rock that is higher than I' (Ps. 61:2). This again struck me so personally with delight. I laughed to myself as this is exactly my new issue – problems with my faint heart.

But even if you don't have literal heart issues, our spiritual heart goes faint because we are so weak. Let us cry (like a tiny baby wanting its mother) from wherever we are to God. We may cry from anywhere – even from the ends of the earth for God hears our cry! What must we cry? We must pray to be led to the Rock. Who masterminds this? The Father. Who leads us? The Holy Spirit. Who is the Rock? Jesus Christ.

He is our Rock and He is in charge of the universe. We see that at the end of the Psalm: the God-man is ruling the universe, enthroned and seated at the right hand of the Father.

What kind of rock do we need? We need one who is infinitely higher than us, who – as we, like shipwrecked, drowning sailors are tossed around in the storms of fear, suffering and death – can haul us out of our sea of troubles.

Blessed Holy Spirit, we cry to you. Lead us to the Rock that is higher than us!

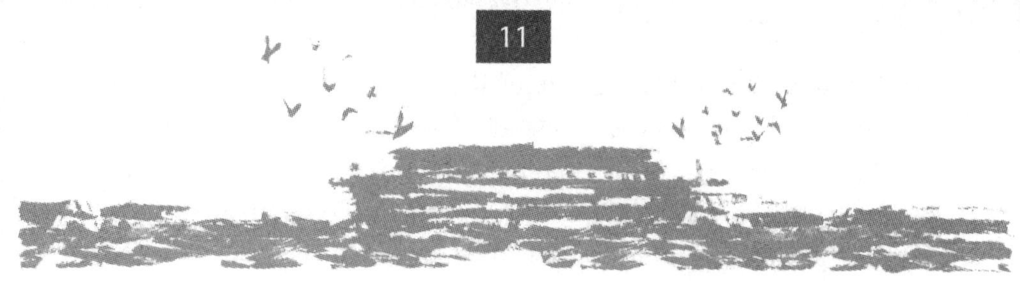

11

Faith in the Storm

MARK 4:35–41

What's our biggest problem as Christians? I suggest it is that we don't know God enough, we don't trust Him enough, we don't love Him enough and we don't pray to Him enough.

This is not a new problem and, in a strange way, we should find that encouraging. Long ago another group of Christians had the same problem – Jesus's disciples. They lived with the Lord for three years and their general slowness should encourage us that God is patient and loving and always seeking to draw us nearer to Himself.

Jesus knew exactly what was coming. He knew there was going to be a storm. He deliberately placed His followers in harm's way. Being close to the Lord is no guarantee of a trouble-free life. Rather, it is the reverse.

God may lead us into suffering so that He can show us more of Himself. As I put it in my own case, 'The cancer cells meant it for harm, but God meant it for good.'

The uncertainty, difficulties for my family, pain, frustrations and fear are all there, but the joy of being involved in the Lord's work, of seeing Him at work in those I've been able to introduce to Christ has been really wonderful. In fact, I've had more opportunities to share my faith in the last seven years than the previous fifty combined.

Where's the ultimate place that we see evil turned to good? When we stand at the foot of the cross. The devil and all the forces of hell meant it for evil, but God used it for our good.

When faced with the storm, I am sure the disciples did all the things that experienced sailors would do: turn the boat into the wind, trim the sails, head for shore, bail out the water – but they didn't do the one blindingly obvious thing they should have done. They did not ask the incarnate God who was right at hand for help. Even when they do ask in desperation, they do so in a rough way.

They say, 'Don't you care?' (Mk. 4:38). How hard it is for them to pray! How small their faith! Likewise, how hard for us to pray and how small our faith can be.

Corrie Ten Boom once said, 'When a Christian shuns fellowship with other Christians, the devil smiles. When he stops studying the Bible, the devil laughs. When he stops praying, the devil shouts for joy.'

But let us be encouraged to pray, for how kind the Lord is towards the disciples. How patient He is. Yes, He reproves them, but He does so out of deep love.

God is so kind and patient towards us despite all our serious shortcomings. 'As a father has compassion on his children, so the LORD has compassion on those who fear him' (Ps. 103:13). God sees all the things that are wrong with us. He sees our laziness, our weak faith, our lack of love, our secret sins, our cold hearts and our prayerlessness. And what does He do? He is full of what the Bible calls in Hebrew 'Chesed', which the Reformers in the sixteenth century translated as 'loving-kindness'.

Out of this loving-kindness comes amazing divine power. Billions and billions of molecules are rearranged and suddenly there is dead calm. Winds may drop but a storm-tossed body of water takes a long time to drop. In a second all is quiet, all is still. Such is the power of the divine Word. It utterly transforms their circumstances.

What is the disciples' reaction? They are even more afraid! What's the answer to fear? More fear! After all, 'The fear of the LORD is the beginning of wisdom' (Ps. 111:10). It begins to dawn on them who this ordinary-looking man asleep in the boat is. When they left the boat they knew Him more than when they got in.

Isn't that what we need? To know the Lord more. To love Him more. To pray to Him more. For as the Puritan preacher Thomas Goodwin says, 'The person who knows Christ best is the person who will pray best.'

12

The Keys of Death

JOHN 11:1–44

The writing of the first Bishop of Liverpool, J.C. Ryle, has been a great source of help to me in my suffering. His famous expository thoughts on the Gospels have been an equal help to many others. Below are seven reflections he made on the story of Lazarus found in John's Gospel. I've added my additional thoughts below each point.

1. 'True Christians may be sick and die.'

   Lazarus gets sick and dies. Why does God allow sickness and death to happen to some people and not to others? I simply don't know. But I do know that 'people are destined to die once, and after that to face judgment' (Heb. 9:27). Being a Christian is no 'get out of jail free card' we can play against suffering and death. What He promises us is not a bypass around suffering but His presence as we go through it.

2. 'Sickness is no sign that God is displeased with us.'

   Nor is there normally a link between suffering and sin. What is important is that suffering can be redemptive and have value if our hope is in Christ.

3. 'Christ is the Christian's best friend. The sisters brought it to his attention. He loves us as well, does he not! None can help like him.'

   How slow I am to act like the sisters. 'None can help like him.' Yes, the creator and ruler of the entire universe knows who we are and, if we are His, loves us with an everlasting and unbreakable love. The sisters bring it to His attention and how wise they are to do that. They don't tell or ask Him to do 'x' or 'y'. They 'bring it to his attention'. Why? Because 'he is the one that he loves', and as Ryle wonderfully notes, 'so are we'.

4. 'Jesus doesn't say that Lazarus will die and I will raise him again. He says enough to stir up hope and faith and prayer, but not enough so that they wouldn't seek God.'

   Suffering is always hard and sometimes it crushes us. Why doesn't God act? Why does He give us half-answers or sometimes no answers? There is no final answer to these questions this side of the grave, but we may say gently that one partial answer may be because He is working His purposes out so that we may know Him better and see His glory.

5. 'The pain of a few is for the benefit of many. Had Jesus just said the word (of healing) none of this would have happened. The pain of one, gloriously, is for the benefit of all (the cross).'

Let us always look at the cross. Whoever and wherever and whenever we are in the dark valley of suffering, the light of the cross shines out. God had a plan to rescue poor, sinful, lost and abandoned humanity and it is a plan which involves suffering. Lazarus's suffering and death prefigures and points us to the cross in the same way that Lazarus's resurrection prefigures and points to Jesus's resurrection. As the master so the servant. We are all called to take up our cross daily and follow Him. God can use our suffering for His glory as He used His Son's suffering.

6. 'How tenderly Christ speaks of the death of believers! "Our friend Lazarus sleeps says the Lord." Every Christian has a friend in heaven of almighty power and boundless love. Lazarus is the friend of Christ even when he is dead. Death is a solemn and miraculous change, but the Christian has nothing to fear. Let us never forget that the grave is the place where the Lord Himself lay and that as he rose again triumphant from that cold bed so also shall all his people. We can boldly say, "I will lay me down in peace and sleep for you Lord alone make me dwell in safety."'

This is simply breathtakingly true. Death is a terrible enemy, but it has been utterly defeated and it is owned by the Lord God Almighty who holds the keys of death. Then finally death itself will be emptied and death itself will be swallowed up and death, in the end, will be no more. So what about us? Shall anything separate us from the owner of life and death? No! We are as much Jesus's friends in death as in life. In fact, far more so because in death we will be with Him and see Him face to face.

7. 'Martha and Mary are very much like us: they had mixed emotions. Certainly, they believed, but they were also troubled and needed to see Jesus more clearly. Jesus draws out these two women's faith. He fans into flame the smouldering embers of the sisters' faith. Martha has good theology, but it's not enough. She needs more of Christ.'

   It is promised in the Old Testament that God does not put out a smouldering and feeble flame (Is. 42:3). That is so encouraging, for that is what we are. Even as Christians we have weak faith and labour slowly with many doubts and fears. Martha has a good theological understanding but she needs much more than that, and so do we. We need to know Christ and His resurrection power.

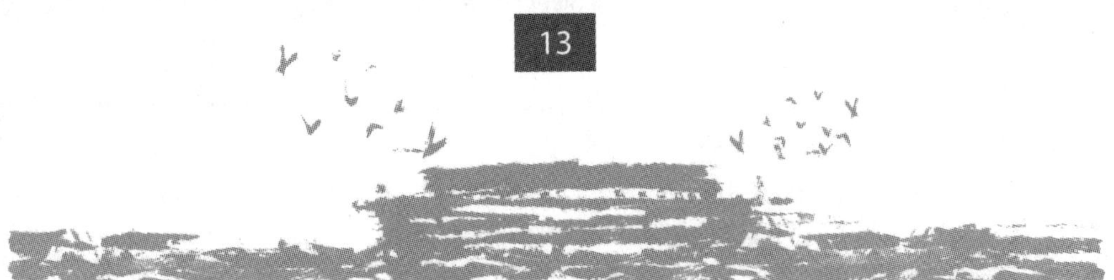

13

The Touch of Life

LUKE 7:11–17

Where do we go for help with fear, suffering and death? The Lord. And what is He like? This is an important point. The better you know someone, the more you are likely to trust them – assuming, that is, that they are of good character.

This small story is one of my favourites for sharing the gospel. We see, first of all, that Jesus meets us at just the right time in our grief and sorrow. Jesus starts the long walk from Capernaum to Nain (about 25 miles) when this young boy is still alive. Perhaps His disciples were puzzled. Why go to that small, out of the way, place? They don't know, but He does. He has an appointment with a grieving widow. She doesn't know who He is, but He knows all about her.

It is the same with us. However utterly insignificant we are. Yet the maker of the universe makes a beeline for us in our suffering. Our eyes may be filled with tears and we can't think of any help, but He is right in front, waiting for us.

We see how perfect God's timing is. A few minutes either way and the two groups of people don't meet. But at just the right time Jesus is there, standing in the way of death. And the people carrying the dead body stand still as they see this ordinary-looking man blocking the procession on its way to dusty death.

What kind of roadblock is this man? He is full of compassion. 'Don't cry' (Lk. 7:13), He says to the grieving mother, whose eyes would doubtless have been full of tears. The original Greek text speaks of Jesus's intestines being twisted. The Lord is deeply moved by our suffering. Though we may think we are forsaken and abandoned, He meets us in our grief. And not just with words; He touches the bier and connects with the dead body. Something no normal Rabbi would do, for it made Him ritually unclean. God is not only moved, He touches us in our suffering. 'I am with you.'

But if our God was only compassionate that would – and I say this reverently – not be enough. For He has equally a colossal life-giving power. Power over death, for at just one word the dead boy is brought back to life immediately.

What is death? Many things, but it is the separation that is the hardest. The boy comes back to life and starts talking! Jesus turns death around 180 degrees. Nain is on a hill so death is carrying off his prey downwards, but Jesus holds the keys of life and death and turns the whole thing around.

So it is with us. Death is a terrible enemy but the Lord owns it. Death will one day be carrying off our body and will also meet Jesus standing in the way. 'Stop! He or she is mine and I am the resurrection and the life', He will say. Death will then have to give up its captives and our bodies will be gloriously resurrected.

In our affliction let us comfort each other with the knowledge of the character of the Lord Jesus and His love for His children. Above all, we need to know and trust Him more. He meets us at just the right time. He is full of compassion and kindness and He touches us in our infirmities. He has total control over death and will raise us all gloriously.

He helped the widow of Nain 2000 years ago. He helps me today. He helps you today and He will help us tomorrow and for all eternity. Alleluia what a Saviour!

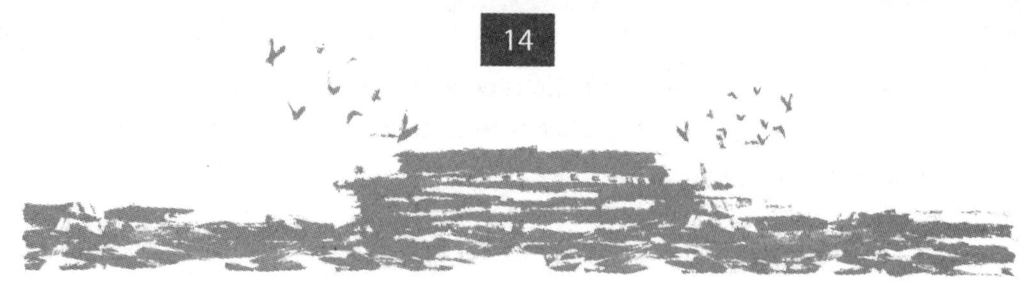

Meeting the Saviour

JOHN 9

We must never treat suffering as an abstract philosophical issue. Jesus's disciples did this in John 9. When they saw a man who was born blind begging they wondered, 'Who sinned, this man or his parents?' Jesus reproves them by saying, 'Neither ... this happened so that the works of God might be displayed in him. As long as it is day, we must do the works of him who sent me. Night is coming, when no one can work' (Jn. 9:2–3).

The Lord was thinking of His own life and death. When Judas leaves to betray Jesus, John writes, 'It was night.' What darkness. This is a passage and verse that has spoken powerfully to me since I've been unwell. As Ryle says in his *Expository Thoughts on the Gospels*, 'There is no work in the grave towards which we are all fast hastening.' The night is coming and this is the day of salvation.

Heaven will be amazing, but it will be too late for evangelism and I feel that imperative strongly. Time is short and we must take every opportunity to tell others of Christ.

What I have also found is that God has not only given me motivation, but also practically helped me in this area in two other ways. Firstly, that suffering opens up an opportunity to shine out the glory of God (Jn. 9:3). People often think that Christians believe they are better than everyone else. But when we are struggling along with fear, suffering and death we are demonstrating that we are precisely not like that. We are vulnerable and weak and, interestingly, people often find commonality in that.

The man born blind, in his troubles, was lying in Jesus's way and so are we. What can we say to others? Well, we can pass on what the blind man was told, 'You have now seen him; in fact, he is the one speaking with you' (Jn. 9:37).

Secondly, how can we help our friends see the Son of Man? Five years ago a Christian friend of mine in the City of London convinced me to try inviting my non-Christian friends to have a chat with me about the Bible. He suggested I use the resource *The Word One To One*, which is simply John's Gospel with helpful discussion notes alongside each verse. I was nervous about doing this but was staggered to find that many of my friends were only too willing to chat with me.

The Word One To One works because the gospel is supernaturally powerful and the notes assist to make each verse accessible. John's Gospel is littered with people who are suffering in one way or another and whose lives are transformed by meeting the Saviour. That's what happens in my experience when I use *The Word One To One*. As I open God's Word with my friends, Jesus steps off the page and starts speaking to them.

Has your faith become all about you without you realising it? You may feel unqualified to share the gospel. Yet, doing so is exactly what we are all called to do in the Great Commission. Of course, there are lots of resources that might help us follow Christ's command, but *The Word One to One* is one that I have found particularly useful.

So many ordinary untrained Christians throughout the world are discovering that God has prepared the hearts of their friends to agree to look at what the Bible has to say. What a wonderful joy it is to become a page-turner and Bible sharer as the Saviour does all the work in bringing new life through His Word.

15

Yet Not My Will

MATTHEW 26:36–46

We are treading here on holy ground and so we must tread reverently.

The Lord Jesus is like us in that He too experienced fear, 'Take this cup away from me; yet not my will, but yours be done' (Lk. 22:42). When we are frightened we may recall that the Lord in His humanity faced fear too. In fact, He faced fear far worse than any of us will ever face.

But He is not like us for He had a choice. Even when He reveals Himself to the soldiers who have come to arrest Him by saying, 'I am he' (Jn. 18:5), this invocation of the divine name causes the soldiers to fall on the ground in terror.

Normally we have no choice in our suffering. The Lord has both the means to escape suffering – one angel is terrifying while a legion would be overwhelming – and the grounds, for He, unlike us, is totally innocent of any wrongdoing. Death has no jurisdiction over Him.

Yet, He is treated as a criminal. He willingly takes the cup of suffering that we deserve, the cup of God's judgment on our sin, and He freely drinks it for the love He has for us.

'My soul is overwhelmed with sorrow to the point of death' (Mt. 26:38). Where does sorrow and suffering come from? From sin. From our sin. Jesus carried our sorrow and our sin to the cross. He is the man of sorrows, which means He is acquainted with sorrow.

Gethsemane shows that Jesus is a man of prayer. Prayer is a confession of our limitation, but Jesus was also God so why did He need to pray? Because, as Philippians 2 tells us, He humbled Himself by taking the nature of a servant.

I find prayer very hard and although my prayer life has improved a little since I've been unwell, I still feel ashamed at how weak it is. How much we can learn from the Lord and His constant prayer. Are we in trouble and frightened of suffering and facing death? Then like the Lord we must ask for help.

'Your will be done', which is, of course, a phrase from The Lord's Prayer. The will of the Father was that Jesus would be the sacrifice for our sins. He alone can pay the bill. We are bankrupt. But how much must we be conformed to Him as He prayed that God's will would be done. He is a man of prayer. His prayer is the prayer of faith. Ours must be the same. He learned obedience in suffering and so must we.

This is hard to do. I don't think it's wrong to pray that God would relieve us from our suffering. But it may be that He will not or, at least, not for a time, or only partly. This is very hard to accept. I know from my own experience. I recently found out that I have to restart chemotherapy. We cannot pray 'yet not my will, but yours be done' by ourselves when we are suffering, but the Spirit can and will help us.

Hugh Martin in his wonderful classic work *The Shadow of Calvary* urges us to join the Lord in Gethsemane, 'Be in prayer beside the saviour, mingling your crying and tears with his: when Jehovah looks on his anointed, he will lift on you the light of his face.'

The way of Christ is the way of the cross. We must go down into the Jordan to come up into the Promised Land. But the Saviour bids us to follow in His footsteps. He has paid the bill which we could not possibly pay and He has drained our cup of suffering and will ferry us safely to the other side.

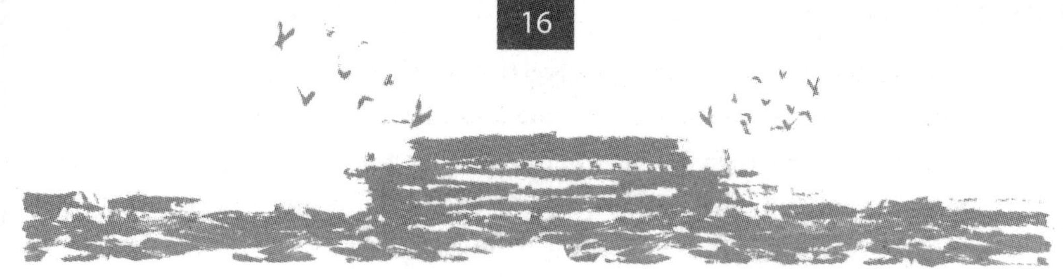

Light in the Valley of Shadows

PSALM 22 — 23

The Psalms are not in a random order. They have been carefully arranged. We must go through the suffering of Psalm 22 to get to the peace and rest of Psalm 23. Not our suffering, but His – Jesus's. Psalm 22 opens with the cry of Jesus on the cross, 'My God, my God, why have you forsaken me?' (Ps. 22:1). He may have recited the entire Psalm for it ends with the last words 'He has done it' or, 'It is finished'.

This is, indeed, holy ground and we can only look on in awe. Martin Luther rightly said, 'God forsaken by God – who can understand it?' Why is He forsaken, alone, His communion with His Father (as to His humanity) interrupted? Because God is too pure to look on evil. He sees the sin that the Son takes and He turns away. That is our sin. We rightly deserve the consequences of sin and even though our suffering is often not the direct consequences of our sin, nonetheless the wages of sin is death.

But there is also amazing balm here for the suffering and fearful. Jesus has stood in our place, rejected and abandoned. If we are in His family then we have a way out of suffering.

In Psalm 22 we see that Jesus, still in His utter abandonment, says twice, 'My God' (Ps. 22:1). Even in His suffering, even when God appears humanly to be far away, He is still our God and He is still mighty to save. He asks questions of God in suffering and so can we. We may often not know why something terrible is happening, but we know that Jesus was abandoned by God so that we will never be abandoned. The cross towers over us casting a mighty light on our way. And where are we going? We are going home.

It's helpful to look at Psalm 23 through the lens of Psalm 22. The entry to our safety is the cross. 'That I may dwell in the house of the LORD all the days of my life' (Ps. 27:4). This life is often a dry desert in which we wander, but the Lord has gone ahead to make a home for us. What a place that will be!

The martyr John Bradford, who was burnt at the stake during the reign of Queen Mary, was reported to have said to the trembling young man being burned with him, 'Be of good comfort brother; for we shall have a merry supper with the Lord this night!'

We are on our way to something mind-blowingly good. While the journey may be hard we can find comfort in God's Word, 'Even though I walk through the darkest valley, I will fear no evil, for you are with me' (Ps. 23:4). When I am at a medical low that verse has repeatedly impressed itself on my mind like a burning light in the valley of the shadow of death.

Each of us must walk through that valley and it is a valley of shadow. It is dark and I know that. There is evil. But in order for there to be a shadow, there must be a light. That light is streaming from the face of Christ. It leads us on and He, the Good Shepherd, is not just ahead holding the door open or behind on the cross having suffered in our place but, perhaps most amazingly of all, He is with us right now. He is walking with us, talking with us, and He has, if you like, two divine sheepdogs with Him called Mercy and Goodness. Evil has to slink away. So the little party, a limping sufferer, a Saviour and two ministering angels struggle on towards glory.

Remember it is 'all the days of my life' (Ps. 27:4). The evil days and the good days; the days of suffering and the days of joy. God in His goodness supplies everything we need in suffering and His mercy on the cross means we don't get what we deserve – eternal suffering and separation from God. Amazingly, rather, we daily receive a free gift – the presence of the Lord God Almighty all the way home.

17

Burning Hearts, Opened Eyes

LUKE 24:13–35

How do many of us feel today? Afraid of death? Depressed and despairing? Maybe we have doubts? What is God going to do when everything seems to be going wrong? Why doesn't He say or do something?

There was a group of people 2000 years ago who felt exactly the same way. When Jesus was arrested, His followers were terrified and ran away. They chose to self-isolate in terror of a cruel execution. Death stalked the streets of Jerusalem as they cowered behind closed doors.

Then after His death on the cross, there is silence from God for three days. God says nothing. The disciples burrow down deeper and deeper into terrified self-isolation. There is no voice from God to comfort or help them. Perhaps they wondered why God was silent.

Then on Sunday morning two of Jesus's disciples, in their doubt and fear of death, decide to go one step further. Jerusalem, where Jesus was crucified is the epicentre of danger for them, so, like many today, they escape from the city and go to the country, to a little village called Emmaus about seven miles walk from Jerusalem. They are running away from fellowship with fellow believers – never a good idea.

As they run away from danger they are depressed and full of doubts. The truth is staring them in the face, but they don't get it. Then something amazing happens. Jesus comes alongside them as they walk along and He speaks to them. They don't recognise Him; their eyes are kept closed as to who He is.

Opening up the Hebrew Bible this mysterious stranger explains to them that the Messiah needed to suffer and die, that there was no other way for humans to get back to God. This is their big blind spot; for them to die on the cross would be pointless. Suffering seems meaningless.

When they get near to their destination Jesus acts as if He is going further. Alarmed, they urge Him to stay with them. Finally, He sits down for a meal and breaks bread with them. At this point, their eyes are opened and they recognise who He is. He then abruptly disappears from their sight.

When they realise who it was who was talking to them they say to one another, 'Were not our hearts burning within us while he talked with us on the road and opened the Scriptures to us?' (Lk. 24:32). They do a U-turn and run back to Jerusalem and find the other disciples and tell them what happened. As they are doing that Jesus appears again and speaks. He says to them all, 'Peace be with you' (Lk. 24:36).

The same thing that happened to the disciples can happen to us. God is here and He is not silent. He speaks to us today. He is, I believe, speaking to you as you read this book.

He speaks to us today in all our troubles and doubts, through His Word, just like He did to the people on the road. And like the disciples on the Emmaus road, as the Word is opened then we, who may also be despondent and suffering, meet the risen Jesus. He steps off the pages of the Bible and into our lives.

What happens when we meet the risen Lord? We realise that both His suffering and ours is part of God's plan. Our faith is strengthened and our doubts disappear. Most of all, our frozen hearts are thawed by the Holy Spirit and start to burn within us as we experience the risen Lord Jesus.

What does Jesus offer us today? The same thing He offered the disciples 2000 years ago. Peace through His death on the cross. Peace with God, with each other and in ourselves. We find peace once we meet the risen Lord.

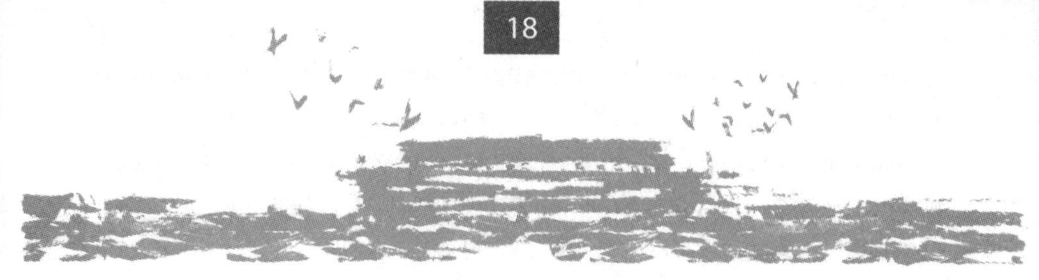

Suffering for the Faith

1 PETER

When I was a young boy my father, who was a pastor, took us Bible smuggling behind the Iron Curtain most summers. When we visited these persecuted churches, I was struck by how vibrant their faith was despite – or perhaps, because of – their suffering.

One man, in particular, a friend of mine called Simo, was often in prison for his faith and yet, even in prison, he couldn't help preaching to his fellow inmates. They were so struck by his example that when the exasperated authorities stuck him in solitary confinement to keep him quiet, the other prisoners demanded he be let out so he could continue to talk to them.

So far in this book, we have looked at general suffering, but sometimes Christian suffer for being Christians. As the gospel spread across the Roman empire, persecution began to grow and we see the result of it in the book of 1 Peter.

The letter reveals that Christians were beginning to face ridicule, which was turning to violence and, soon after, death. Peter tells his readers not to be surprised by suffering. In fact, if they are insulted they are blessed 'for the Spirit of glory and of God rests on you'

(1 Pet. 4:14). This was what happened to my friend Simo. The glory of God rested on him.

My own church leader has written on these verses, 'Rather than suffering clouding the believer's current experience of God, it is a sign of God's glorious presence with them.'

We must be willing to suffer for Christ 'because Christ suffered for you, leaving an example, that you should follow in his steps' (1 Pet. 2:21). In many parts of the world today, Christians suffer daily, even to death. And, even in the UK, where Christianity has had (exceptionally) a privileged position in recent history, this is changing. Not, of course, to the extent that we risk the persecution of life behind the Iron Curtain, but certainly through ridicule and discrimination.

Churches – and especially – their leaders, who hold to the teaching of Scripture often face fierce opposition in their wider communities. Please pray for them, that they would continue to stand faithfully for orthodox belief.

We should return good for evil towards those who persecute us. Peter tells us that we should commit ourselves to God and 'continue to do good' (1 Pet. 4:19). The examples of Christians' patient endurance often turns persecutors to Christ. Think of the apostle Paul, or other examples throughout history. Many of the Khmer Rouge leaders, who beat Christians to death in the killing fields of Cambodia, found forgiveness in Christ.

Suffering for the cause of Christ is brief. How short this life is and how transient are our trials. As Peter says, 'the God of all grace ... after you have suffered a little while, will himself restore you and make you strong, firm and steadfast' (1 Pet. 5:10). May that be so for us.

19

The Medicine Chest

Finally, then, to the medicine chest: what does the Bible have to say about suffering? If there is a God who is loving, why does He allow suffering?

Firstly, suffering wasn't part of God's plan.

The world was made by God and it was very good. There was no suffering or death. Suffering results from the Fall; human beings deliberately deciding, when presented with a choice, to choose evil.

Secondly, God allows suffering.

Bad things happen to good people. The book of Job is a mysterious book that deals head-on with the question of suffering. It shows us that God is in control of everything, including evil.

Christopher Ash points out that Job's friends wrongly reason like this: God is fair and gives us what we deserve. Therefore, if you are suffering, you have done something wrong.

Job (whom we know hasn't done anything particularly wrong) is unsurprisingly unimpressed by this train of thought and replies with a different conclusion: I am suffering. I haven't done anything wrong. Therefore God is unfair.

God eventually answers Job out of a storm, but He only gives Him a partial answer. We can see the big picture behind God's purposes while Job can't. Job continuously complains about what is happening to him and says, 'Oh, that my words were recorded, that they were written on a scroll' (Job 19:23). Which, of course, is ironically exactly what did happen.

But that wasn't any help to Job at the time and, in that sense, we are all like Job. We are in the suffering story and struggle to see any reason for it. When we meet God, everything, I believe, will click into place. But how to live in the meantime?

Job sensed his need for a person to help with his suffering, a friend, an advocate, and a mediator. Someone to represent him, help him and get alongside him.

Now, finally, here comes the good news for all of us experiencing suffering. God didn't leave us to the consequences of our own sin and to deal with suffering on our own, but He intervened, came on a rescue mission and offered us a way out of suffering. And that rescue mission involved God Himself suffering.

Thirdly, Luke records what Jesus prays just before He was arrested and crucified, 'Father, if you are willing, take this cup from me; yet not my will, but yours be done' (Lk. 22:42). Luke continues the narrative, 'An angel from heaven appeared to him and strengthened him. And being in anguish, he prayed more earnestly, and his sweat was like drops of blood falling to the ground' (Lk. 22:44).

When we look at our own suffering, there is nowhere else to go but the cross. We must always end up at the cross. We can't make sense of our suffering without looking at God's suffering on the cross.

Dietrich Bonhoeffer was a German pastor who protested against the persecution of the Jews by the Nazis. As a result, he was sent to a concentration camp and was executed on Hitler's order just before the war ended. Shortly before this, he smuggled out of his cell a scrap of paper with these words, 'Only a suffering God can help us.'

God can suffer because He became human and therefore experienced the types of suffering that we also face. Truly, this is mind-blowing. The infinite God, who made the universe, is also a personal God whom we may very reverently say 'knows what it's like' to suffer.

God chooses to redeem the world through suffering Himself. God, therefore, knows what it's like to suffer, but He does it voluntarily because He is perfect. I have no choice over my suffering, it just happens to me. Of course, if I did I would stop suffering straight away and so would anyone sensible. But God chose, in the person of the Son of God, Jesus Christ, to suffer.

Why did He do this? Because He loves us.

We could also add that God deeply sympathises with us in our suffering. Jesus wept at the tomb of Lazarus. But He also does something about our suffering. He comes on a rescue mission and by suffering freely, He opens up a way of escape from the evil that causes those who suffer.

Fourthly, '"He will wipe every tear from their eyes. There will be no more death" or mourning or crying or pain, for the old order of things has passed away.' He who was seated on the throne said, "I am making everything new!"' (Rev. 21:4–5).

We can all picture a small toddler who trips in the garden, scuffs her knee and runs crying to her father. He sits her on his knee, takes care of the graze, pulls a tissue out of his pocket and wipes away his daughter's tears. The toddler is comforted and soon stops crying and runs off to play.

This is the amazing and staggering image that we find right at the end of the Bible. God Himself will wipe away all our tears and pain. All suffering and pain and even, I suggest, the memory of suffering will be removed. Everything that's gone wrong will be made right. Evil itself will be defeated and destroyed.

How is this possible? Through Jesus's death on the cross. Why? Because He loves us.

What should our response be? Trust in the suffering servant, the Lord Jesus Christ.

20

Death of Death[7]

REVELATION

We opened this book by thinking about three intruders: fear, suffering and death. One of them, death, is inescapable. Death is the last enemy and it is a terrible one. But we have hope, for we have one who has conquered death, 'Christ was raised from the dead, he cannot die again; death no longer has mastery over him' (Rom. 6:9).

What a glorious truth. And there is more, for Christ has dominion over death, 'I am the Living One; I was dead, and now look, I am alive for ever and ever! And I hold the keys of death and Hades' (Rev. 1:18). To have the keys to something is to own it. Yes, the Lord owns death and hell. And what will He do with it? He will destroy it.

The prophet Isaiah declares, 'On this mountain he will destroy the shroud that enfolds all peoples, the sheet that covers all nations; he will swallow up death forever. The Sovereign Lord will wipe away the tears from all faces' (Is. 25:7–8). This is going to happen, 'Then death and Hades were thrown into the lake of fire' (Rev. 20:14).

---

7 This chapter was originally published in amended form as a blog post: http://jsjmarshall.blogspot.com/2020/04/dr-martyn-lloyd-jones-on-preparing-for.html?m=1

So the end is sure, but, in the meantime, how do we face the last enemy? Dr Martyn Lloyd-Jones was a famous Welsh preacher of the last century and he said this, 'We all have to die – that is a fact, it is common sense. But where does Christianity come in? The Christian is not afraid of death because he has the assurance that he will not be left alone.' Then Lloyd-Jones focused on the parable of Dives and Lazarus and the verse 'the beggar died and the angels carried him to Abraham's side' (Lk. 16:22). The angels, he said, came:

> *I believe in the ministry of angels and think of it more and more. Death is not parting only, but more, it is meeting, and though it is an experience we have never passed through we have the assurance that nothing can separate us from the love of Christ and that at death we will meet with Him.*

He spoke of an old man. Lloyd-Jones was visiting him on his deathbed, and the man was at the extremity of life and suddenly he threw up his arms and his face shone, and he was already meeting the Lord before he had gone. Lloyd-Jones added:

> *We are going to be with Christ ... Our greatest trouble is that we really don't believe the Bible ... exactly what it says – exceeding great and precious promises. We think we know it, but we do not really appropriate this and actually believe it is true. Here we have no continuing city. Our light affliction is but for a moment. We have to take these statements literally. They are facts, they are not merely ideas.*

Each one of us must die and the River Jordan – the biblical picture of death – is a hard, hard river to cross. We shall find it deeper or shallower as we believe in the King of the place. But what glory awaits us on the other side! John Bunyan reveals a wonderful insight into this trail in his book *Pilgrim's Progress* when Mr Steadfast says:

> *I see myself now at the end of my Journey, my toilsome days are ended. I am going now to see that Head that once was crowned with thorns, and that face that was spit upon for me. I have formerly lived by hearsay and faith, but now I go where I shall live by sight, and shall be with him in whose company I delight myself. I have loved to hear my Lord spoken of; and wherever I have seen the print of his shoe on the earth, there I have coveted to set my foot too. His name to me has been a civet-box; yea sweeter than all perfume. His voice to me has been most sweet; and his countenance I have more desired than they that have most desired the light of the sun. His Word I did use to gather for my food, and for antidotes against my faintings. He has held me, and hath kept me from mine iniquities; yea, my steps hath he strengthened in his Way ... Glorious it was to see how the open region was filled with horses and chariots, with trumpeters and pipers ... to welcome the pilgrims as they went up, and followed one another in at the Beautiful Gate of the City.*

Dear friend, see you in the City. The Lord will never leave us alone on our journey home. If we are His, He will bring us safely to the other side and we will see Him face to face and He will wipe away every tear.

In the meantime, let us love to see the print of His shoe and to hear His voice and the sound of His name!

Appendix

These devotions are designed to be a helpful introduction to what the Bible has to say about how we can have hope in a suffering world. If you have not read much of the Bible before, or are unfamiliar with the stories in this book, here is a very short overview of where they come from in the Bible:

'The Intruder', 'All Aboard' and 'Thorns and Roses' take place in Genesis, the first book in the Bible and part of the Old Testament, which is shared by Jews and Christians. The first part of Genesis covers the period before human history and tells us of a Creator God who made the universe good. Evil entered the world when humans chose to disobey God, which led to their exile from God's presence ('The Intruder'). Things went from bad to worse and God sent a flood to wipe out humanity, rescuing only Noah and his family ('All Aboard').

The second part of Genesis begins in the Bronze Ages in the Middle East with a man called Abraham who was told by God to go and live in Canaan (modern-day Israel). His great-grandson Joseph was sold into slavery by his brothers but became ruler of Egypt and saved his family from famine ('Thorns and Roses').

Job ('The Best Medicine') is probably the oldest book in the Bible. Job tells the story of a man who lost all that he had in a series of tragedies. The book is a dialogue between Job and his friends, Job's comforters, about what is causing Job's terrible suffering. At the end God speaks to Job from a storm, silencing their debates.

'The Rollercoaster', 'In His Hand', 'The Undistracted Parent', 'Rock in a Sea of Troubles' and 'Light in the Valley of the Shadow of Death' are taken from the Psalms, a collection of 150 poems, designed to be sung. The main author, who wrote at least half of these poems, was King David, who was the King of Israel in around 1000 BC.

After David, the kingdom split into two, Israel in the north and Judah in the south. 'God on the Throne' is from 2 Kings which tells of Naaman the commander of the armies of Syria (who were called Arameans). They were in conflict with the northern kingdom of Israel, which had mainly turned away from God.

The largest number of devotions are from the four 'gospels' (literally 'good news') in the New Testament.

Christians believe that the Old Testament promises a Messiah, a Saviour who will come, and that the New Testament tells of the coming of that Messiah, Jesus Christ (Christ means Messiah in Greek). Jesus was born in Israel, which was then part of the Roman Empire, in approximately 0 BC.

'Faith in the Storm', 'The Keys of Death', 'The Touch of Life', 'Meeting the Saviour', 'Yet Not My Will' and 'Burning Hearts, Opened Eyes' come from the four gospel accounts written by Matthew, Mark, Luke and John. Matthew and John were two of Jesus's twelve disciples or followers and recorded the events they saw. Mark and Luke came shortly afterwards and interviewed eyewitnesses of Jesus's life and times. All four were written within a very short period after the events of Jesus's life and tell us in rich detail about His birth, life, miracles, teaching, arrest, trial, crucifixion, death, resurrection and return to heaven. If you want to explore Christianity further I suggest you start with one of them, ideally with a Christian friend who can answer any questions. You could also try The Word One to One resource, which is John's Gospel plus explanatory notes: https://www.theword121.com/

Within a few years, the Christian message spread like wildfire throughout the Roman Empire. One of Jesus's followers, Peter, wrote a letter in the second half of the first century to some of these early Christians. They were experiencing persecution and suffering because of what they believed and Peter wrote to help them in these tough times ('Suffering for the Faith').

Finally, we get to the last book in the New Testament, Revelation ('Death of Death'). This was written in a similar context to Peter's, beginning with short letters to churches in modern-day Turkey. Most of the book is a series of visions, which can be hard to understand, but show us that God is in control of everything. We see that human history is moving to a conclusion where Jesus will return and all humanity, alive or dead, will be judged by God, and those who trust in Jesus will live with Him forever in his glorious City.

I hope these devotions encourage you to read more of the Bible and discover the only real hope we have in the face of death.

Also available by Jeremy Marshall

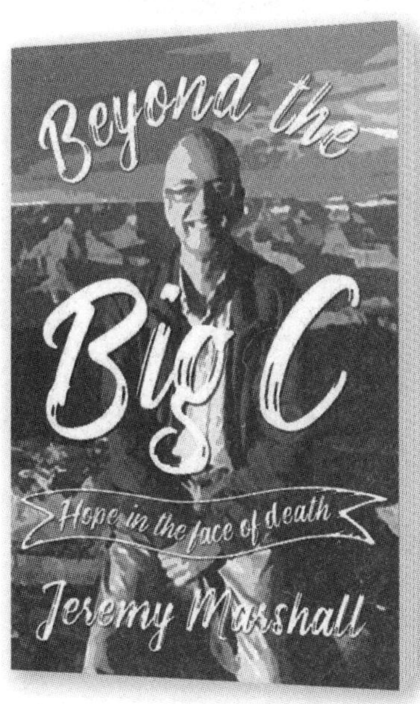

Beyond the Big C

Jeremy Marshall was diagnosed with a rare form of cancer in 2013. He was 49 years old, happily married with three children. After undergoing surgery and a course of radiotherapy, Jeremy was declared cancer-free. But three years later he was diagnosed with cancer again, this time in a different form and was told it was incurable.

Beyond the Big C chronicles Jeremy's extraordinary relationship with cancer and, more than anything, his extraordinary relationship with the person who promises life beyond the prognosis. The essence of Jeremy's story is that despite the sickness and disease present in the world, a life lived in light of Christ's death on the cross means there is hope for the future no matter what.

Jeremy Marshall is the former CEO of the UK's oldest private bank, C. Hoare & Co. He was diagnosed with terminal cancer in 2016.

HOPE
in the face of
suffering
20 daily devotions
for tough times
Jeremy Marshall

10 Publishing
a division of 10 of those.com